"THE WORLD'S EASIEST POCKET GUIDE"

— TO —

Planning Your First Investment

"THE WORLD'S EASIEST POCKET GUIDE"

— TO —

Planning Your First Investment

LARRY BURKETT

WITH TODD MARTIN
ILLUSTRATED BY KEN SAVE

MOODY PRESS
CHICAGO

For Lightwave Publishing
Managing Editor: *Rick Osborne*
Project Assistant: *Mikal Marrs, Ed Strauss*
Text Director: *Christie Bowler*
Art Director: *Terry van Roon*

Text & Illustrations © 2001 BURKETT & KIDS, LLC
Executive Producer: *Allen Burkett*

ISBN: 0-8024-0993-8

1 3 5 7 9 10 8 6 4 2

Printed in the United States of America

Table of Contents

How to Use This Book

Shortly after leaving home, many teens and young adults embark on a learning curve so drastic that it resembles a roller-coaster ride. Things they never did before—such as holding down a full-time job, paying bills, saving money, renting an apartment, using a credit card—suddenly become sink-or-swim survival skills. Most people fail to learn these basics while still at home and are woefully unprepared for life in the real world when they move out on their own.

The first four books in this series—*Getting Your First Credit Card, Buying Your First Car, Renting Your First Apartment,* and *Preparing for College*—were written to teach you the basic life skills you need to survive in today's jungle. In these four new books, *Your First Full-Time Job, Your First Savings Plan, Your First Investment,* and *Your First Financial Plan,* we walk you step-by-step through getting and keeping a job, saving money, investing money without losing your shirt, and getting and keeping control of your money.

These books contain a wealth of commonsense tips. They also give sound advice from a godly, biblical perspective. It is our prayer that the books in this series will save you from having to learn these things in the "school of hard knocks."

To get the most out of these books, you should photo-copy and complete the checklists and forms we've included. We provided them to help you take on these new tasks step-by-step and to make these books as practical as possible.

Each book contains a glossary to explain commonly used terms. If at any point while reading you need a clear definition of a certain word or term, you can look it up. Each book also contains a helpful index that allows you to find pages where a key word or subject is mentioned in the book.

CHAPTER 1

Why Invest?

Why Invest?

In a society in which material wealth and possessions are so important, it is vital to step back and reflect on principles of money management recorded thousands of years ago in the Bible.

First, you need to understand that your most important investment is a relationship with God through Jesus Christ. It is impossible to serve two masters. You must choose between the pursuit of happiness and fulfillment through money or through God. If you can put these two potential masters in perspective, God promises to provide all you need to serve Him.

Reasons for Investing

God's number one prerequisite for investing is always centered on attitude and motivation. The goal of saving and investing is to provide for you and your family's needs, to provide a comfortable lifestyle, and to use the rest to help others. Take time to reflect on what would make a comfortable—not extravagant—lifestyle for you. Physical things will never give you satisfaction. The sooner you come to grips with that, the more satisfying your life will be.

As a young Christian, you need to ask yourself what your motivation for investing is and what you should do with any surplus from the investments, in light of God's principles. God is not against you having money. He doesn't want you to live in rags or in a dump, but He hates the evil attitudes that often accompany wealth. There are good and not-so-good reasons for investing. If you are investing for lousy reasons, it's like having your ladder leaning against the wrong building. No matter how high you climb, you still end up on the wrong building.

Good Reasons for Investing

Here are three scripturally sound reasons for investing.

1. *Meet future needs.* The Bible teaches that people have the responsibility to work and provide for their needs as well as for the needs of their family. God knows that you and your family will need money before you have even thought of it.

2. *Multiply to give more.* The parable of the talents shows that God wants increase so that more money can go back to do His work.

3. *Further the gospel and fund special needs.* Every week when the collection is taken up at church, wouldn't it be great to put in more than the loose change you found in the couch? Not only do you need to set up a budget for giving, you need to find ways to give even more. Investing wisely is one of those ways.

So what is God's goal for your investments, you ask? It's simple and straightforward. It is to provide for your future needs, to enable you to give to those who are less fortunate, and to enable you to have money to support His kingdom work.

Not-So-Good Reasons for Investing

1. *Greed.* Greed is the desire to continually have more and demand only the best (1 Timothy 6:9).

2. *Envy.* Envy is the desire to achieve based on other people's successes (Psalm 73:3). If you feel the need to keep up with the Joneses, maybe envy has a hold on you.

3. *Pride.* Pride is the desire to be elevated because of material achievements (1 Timothy 6:17). If wealth can make you feel important, its lack will leave you feeling like nothing.

4. *Ignorance.* Ignorance is following the counsel of other misguided people because of lack of discernment (Proverbs 14:7). Many people have lost a lot of money due to a "sure win" investment.

How Much Should You Invest?

At this point you probably don't have money bursting out of your pockets, so just being able to invest is a bonus. Before you actually have the money, it is important to decide how much to give to the work of God and what you are going to do with it. Making the decision ahead of time takes much of the conflict and temptation away when you're holding the money in your hot little hand. One way to take care of this is to set a percentage figure of any investment increase aside for giving. Then, when you receive any income, interest, dividends, or return from your investments, you give that percentage of it to the ministries or people you have decided to help and do what you want with the rest, such as reinvest it.

The information in this book is intended to take you from being an investment rookie to a Wall Street tycoon! Or at least someone who knows the basics and can begin making the first investment.

Take time right now to decide how much of your investment increase you will give away and record it here.

I will give away _____% of any investment increase or return I receive.

Three Fundamental Investment Concepts

You're going to learn three essential steps to successful investing.

5   10   15   20   25
Years Until Retirement

1. ACT NOW
Time is an investor's best friend. As an example, by starting to invest $500 a month at age 40, you could have $475,000 by age 65. If you wait until you're 45, you'll have less than $300,000. That's a 38 percent penalty for waiting just five years.*

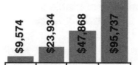

$10 $25 $50 $100
Monthly Savings over 25 Yrs.

2. SAVE MORE
Due to the power of compounding, even a small increase in your monthly savings rate now can make a big difference over time.*

4%   6%   8%   10%
Annual Rate of Return
over 25 Years

3. INVEST BETTER
You don't have to receive a windfall to make a big difference in your retirement income. Just a slightly higher rate of return can make a big difference in a $10,000 investment.*

* The hypothetical examples shown assume a fixed rate of return of continuing investments of 8 percent, except where noted.

Source—Oppenheimer Investments

CHAPTER 2

Saving versus Investing

Saving versus Investing

For the first time in the history of the United States, over 50 percent of households currently invest in the stock market, either individually or through employee-related savings programs. That staggering number does not include all the people who invest in precious gems, metals, fine art, collectibles, real estate, or Pokemon cards.

Saving is the act of setting aside a portion of your money for purposes in the future. Investing puts those savings to work to increase them for that future use. When you put money in your piggy bank, you are saving. When you break the piggy bank open, take the money to the bank, and earn interest on it, you become an investor.

The second major difference between saving and investing is how your money increases. When most people think of saving, they think of a savings account at a bank: a place to put their money and keep it safe. An even more drastic view of savings might be sticking your money in a shoebox or under your mattress.

Banks often pay a very low interest rate on savings accounts, usually lower than the current rate of inflation. What that means is that your money is growing slower than the cost of things, like a new stereo, is increasing. So if you put enough money in your savings account to buy a new stereo now, in five years you won't have enough to buy that stereo.

People invest in stocks, bonds, mutual funds, land, gold, or collectibles because they feel that the value of their investment will go up over time, usually *faster* than inflation.

The different approaches to what to do with your money can be illustrated by comparing what typically happens to the value of $500 set aside per month.

Return %	1 Year	2 Years	3 Years	4 Years	5 Years
0%	$6,000	$12,000	$18,000	$24,000	$ 36,000
5%	$6,829	$15,592	$26,840	$41,275	$ 85,573
8%	$7,397	$18,418	$34,835	$59,294	$150,030
10%	$7,808	$20,655	$41,799	$76,570	$227,936
12%	$8,247	$23,334	$50,457	$99,915	$352,992

You can see what happens when you save in one of two ways. By burying your money in the backyard, you end up with exactly how much you put in: $36,000. This is a great start, but look at it compared to digging it up and doing something with it: If you put your money in a savings account at the bank and earn 5 percent interest (probably more than you really could), your money after thirty years more than doubles what is hidden in your backyard.

Now look at what happens when you invest your money in something like stocks, bonds, or mutual funds, the main types of investments: Although each of these investments vary in the type of return they give, and may even lose value, they have all averaged much better than savings accounts. Over the past 75 years, stocks have averaged about an 11 percent return and bonds about 7 percent. At 10 percent return on average, investing in stocks and bonds would be worth over six times what the money in your backyard would be worth after five years (assuming you could remember where it was buried!).

Use Your Talents

In the parable of the talents (Matthew 25:14–30), Jesus uses a story about what we do with our money as an illustration of what we should do with what God has given us. In the story, three people were given different amounts of money by their boss (in the form of talents) to take care of while he was gone, based on what the boss thought they could handle.

The employees who had been given five and two talents doubled them. The third employee had taken his one talent and buried it in the backyard because he was afraid to lose it.

This parable has some powerful points about investing. First, the boss expected some return on his money.

Second, the wise employees doubled their money by going *at once* and *putting it to work*. Notice the twofold approach. One, you start right away because time is your greatest asset. Two, put your money to work. A wise investor sees money as a tool to increase resources rather than as a master to serve.

Let's illustrate this by looking at what happens to two college graduates. Joe Graduate lands his first job and in celebration he buys a brand-new car. He takes out a loan that will only cost $2,000 a year. After four years of car payments, Joe is married with one child and needs a bigger car. Since he hasn't been able to save, he borrows the money, which again costs only $2,000 a year.

While Joe was buying his new car, Sue Scholar took public transit until she could save up for a used car. After only two years, she had enough for a good used car and was able to set away $2,000 per year for savings and investments. She maintained her used car well and did not have to buy a new one so was able to continue to set aside $2,000 per year. Now, eight years after graduation, Sue has a nice nest egg that she has been putting to work for the future. After the same eight years, Joe decides he has to get serious about saving and investing $2,000 a year. Look what happens to Sue, who put her money to work, and Joe, the later investor who was working for his money.

	Sue Scholar		Joe Graduate	
Age	Payment	End of Year	Payment	End of Year
22	$2,000	$2,240	$0	$0
23	$2,000	$4,749	$0	$0
24	$2,000	$7,559	$0	$0
25	$2,000	$10,706	$0	$0
26	$2,000	$14,230	$0	$0
27	$2,000	$18,187	$0	$0
28	$0	$20,359	$2,000	$2,240
29	$0	$22,802	$2,000	$4,749
30	$0	$25,539	$2,000	$7,559
35	$0	$45,008	$2,000	$27,551
40	$0	$79,320	$2,000	$62,785
60	$0	$765,140	$2,000	$767,042
65	$0	$1,348,438	$2,000	$1,363,780
Total Invested	$12,000		$76,000	

Based on 12% annual growth in a tax-deferred account

Jesus' key principles regarding investing are: First, you need to start as soon as possible because time is your ally. Second, don't just save your money but put your money to work for you by investing wisely. When your money starts working for you, it is like hiring an extra worker whose pay goes to you! The Bible reminds us that the borrower is slave to the lender. In other words borrowers are working to pay back their money while wise investors are putting their money to work for them.

CHAPTER 3

Climbing the Ladder of Risk

Climbing the Ladder of Risk

When it comes to investing, the scariest word has to be "risk." "What if I lose all my money? What if my investment goes down?"

Investment Risks

Investing does carry risks and every potential investor needs to understand them. Risk is usually measured on the guaranteed return of the principal, not how much earnings the investment might yield. The "principal" is what you initially invest. The "return" is how much money you make per year off that principal. And the "yield" is the amount of return expressed as a percentage. So the risk discussed here is the potential to lose the money you started with.

United States Government Treasury bills, bonds, and notes (see chapter 6) are the lowest risk of all investments because they are backed by the U.S. government. Measuring and defining risk is crucial to investing. The greater the risk of losing your money, the greater the reward you expect; the less risk, the less reward or return you expect. Since U.S. Treasury bills, bonds, and notes offer the least risk, they can offer the least interest rate reward or return. This means that we can equate rate or return with risk. The lower the risk of losing your money, the lower the rate of return paid. The higher the risk, the higher the rate has to be.

Although it is generally true that the greater the risk, the greater the reward, it is not so simple. The goal of a good investment is to maximize the potential return while minimizing the potential risk. If you come across a rate of return dramatically different from similar investments—say someone offers a great return and says there is no risk—ask if he or she has any land for sale in the Everglades! If it sounds too good to be true, it probably is.

Risk Tolerance

The ability to deal with risk is "risk tolerance": How much can the value of your investment drop and you still get a good night's sleep? Risk tolerance varies from person to person and depends on factors like your age and how soon you might need your money. Generally, the younger you are and the longer you have to invest before need-ing the money, the greater the risk you may be willing to take.

If you have trouble dealing with a drop in your investments' value, you should stick with something that guarantees the safety of your principal. But if your investment is very safe, it may not increase enough to meet your future needs—and that too is a risk. If you have the stomach to ride out the ups and downs of financial market fluctuations, you may be able to seek higher returns.

The Risk Ladder

Here is a general overview of investments from least to most risky. The most important types are covered in detail later.

Lower Risk Investments

- *Certificates of Deposit,* or CDs, can be purchased for specific amounts and pay a fixed rate of return. You need to leave your money in the CD a set length of time. That means you may pay a penalty for cashing the CD in early. Think of a CD as a deposit at the bank that you say you will not touch for a specific period of time. The bank knows you will not withdraw that money tomor-row so they can loan it out and charge higher interest rates than they are paying you. This means they can pay you more interest on your deposit than if you just left it in your savings account.

- *U.S. Savings Bonds* are the result of loaning Uncle Sam a little cash. There are several types, the most common being EE, HH, and I bonds. If the government comes out with O bonds, you could have an "E-HI-E-HI-O" bond collection! Bonds are pur-chased for 50 percent of their face value or what they are worth when they mature. So a $500 bond costs $250; when it matures it will be worth $500. You can buy these bonds for as little as $25 for a $50 bond that matures in eight to twelve years.

- *U.S. Treasuries.* The U.S. government seeks loans in the form of bills, notes, and bonds. Since the government does not always have the money to pay its expenses, it borrows from you. The only difference in bills, notes, and bonds is the length of matu-rity for each. These are usually sold in multiples of $1,000, $5,000, or $10,000.

Higher Risk Investments

Once you get beyond government guaranteed investments, you move up the risk ladder. Higher risk investments include stocks, corporate and municipal bonds, mutual funds, real estate, and collectibles. The list from the least to greatest risk looks like this:

- *Corporate and Municipal Bonds,* like their U.S. government namesakes, are loans made to businesses and states or municipalities to finance projects. Schools, hospitals, and new power plants are usually financed by bonds. Think of them as IOUs that these companies or municipalities owe you.

- *Mutual Funds* are the pooled monies of many different investors. You own a piece of the pot that is then invested in stocks or bonds. Your share value goes up or down based on the value of all the items owned by the pot.

- *Stocks* represent ownership in the company that issues it. You can't buy a $5 billion company outright, but you can own a piece of it. Realistically, you might own a couple of nuts and bolts on a machine that makes snowmen out of cotton balls. If that company makes money, you share in it. If it loses money, you share in the losses.

Greed or God

Over the past 75 years the typical return in the stock market has been around 11 percent. Over the past decade that number has been closer to 17 percent. With return rates climbing, investors are becoming less satisfied with normal returns and, consequently, normal risk. People are greedy by nature and want it all now.

In spite of all that is written in God's Word against excessive risk taking, many Christians violate biblical principles and take such risks for three basic reasons.

1. *A desire to "get rich quick."* Proverbs 23:4–5 says, "Do not wear yourself out to get rich; have the wisdom to show restraint. Cast but a glance at riches, and they are gone, for they will surely sprout wings and fly off to the sky like an eagle."

   Next time you get lured into a get-rich-quick scheme, remember the basic rules that God's Word teaches on "get rich quick."

   - Don't get involved with things you do not understand. Proverbs 24:3–4 says, "By wisdom a house is built, and through understanding it is established; through knowledge its rooms are filled with rare and beautiful treasures."

- Don't risk money you cannot afford to lose. Ecclesiastes 5:14 says, "When those riches were lost through a bad investment and he had fathered a son, then there was nothing to support him" (NASB).
- Don't make a quick decision. Get-rich-quick schemes try to create a panic about time running out and the chance of a lifetime.

2. *A desire to make up for waiting too long.* Many people, like Joe Graduate in chapter 2, suddenly realize time is slipping by and they haven't invested anything. Start young and let the best-kept investment secret work for you: *Compound Interest!*

In order to understand compounding, ask yourself if you would rather be given $100,000 or one cent doubled each day for a month? Calculate it yourself before you choose.

When you double your investment, you are compounding it so that it begins to increase exponentially. To figure out how long it takes to double your money, use the Rule of 72: Divide 72 by the interest rate. The answer gives you the number of years it takes to double your money. If you were getting 8 percent interest on an investment, your money would double in $72 \div 8 = 9$ years. If you were getting 7.2 percent, it would double in 10 years.

The cost of waiting too long is not just less return. It's too much risk. Most people who start investing for retirement too late try to make up for lost time by taking a higher risk. The higher risk may produce higher returns, but there is no guarantee.

3. *Taking excessive risk through ignorance.* Proverbs 13:15 says, "Good understanding wins favor, but the way of the unfaithful is hard." People seldom knowingly take extra risk through investments. Most who do take it out of ignorance rather than by design.

Determining Your Risk Tolerance

Before you consider any type of investment, it is important to understand your tolerance for risk. Your answers to the following questions show whether you are a conservative, moderate, or aggressive investor. You'll use the results at the end of the next chapter to help you put an appropriate mix of investments together that are in line with your tolerance for risk.

Circle the answer that most closely matches your own investment philosophy, add up your score, and record it here.

My Risk Tolerance: Total = _____ points.

1. *My investment is for the long term. The end result is more important than how I go about achieving it.*
   a. I totally disagree. *(1 point)*
   b. I can accept some variability but not losses of principal. *(2 points)*
   c. I can accept reasonable amounts of price fluctuation in total return. *(3 points)*
   d. I can accept an occasional year of negative performance in the interest of increasing my investment. *(4 points)*
   e. I totally agree. *(5 points)*

2. *What is the importance of current income to you?*
   a. Essential and the exact dollar amount per year must be known. *(1 point)*
   b. Essential but willing to accept uncertainty about the amount. *(2 points)*
   c. Important but there are other factors to consider. *(3 points)*
   d. Modest current income is desirable. *(4 points)*
   e. I am investing to increase my investments for the future and am not concerned about current income. *(5 points)*

3. *What is the amount of decline you can accept in a current three-month period?*
   a. None. *(1 point)*
   b. A little but not for the entire year. *(2 points)*
   c. Consistency of results is more important than outstanding performance. *(3 points)*
   d. A few quarters of decline is a small price to pay to be invested when the stock market takes off. *(4 points)*
   e. Unimportant. *(5 points)*

4. *What is the importance of beating inflation?*
   a. Not losing any money and getting an income are more important. *(1 point)*
   b. Willing to beat inflation but other investment needs come first. *(3 points)*
   c. Essential to ensure that you get a real return on your investment. *(5 points)*

5. *What is the importance of beating the stock market over the economic cycle (5–7 years) to you?*
   a. Irrelevant. *(1 point)*
   b. I prefer consistency over superior results. *(3 points)*
   c. Critical. *(5 points)*

Source: Lipper Inc.

CHAPTER 4

Don't Put All Your Eggs in One Basket

Don't Put All Your Eggs in One Basket

Solomon may well be the richest man who ever lived, and he is also described as the wisest. In Ecclesiastes 11:2 he gave this advice about investing, "Give portions to seven, yes to eight, for you do not know what disaster may come upon the land." This concept has been known for generations as, "Don't put all your eggs in one basket."

Regardless of how young you might be, what your income level, time horizon (time until you need the money), or personality is, you must diversify your investments. Diversifying is when you do not put all your investable dollars in the same focused investment. Diversification takes many forms: (1) Among asset classes; stocks are one kind of asset class, and bonds are another type of asset class. (2) Among different areas of the economy, such as technology and health care. (3) Among different regions and economies of the world, such as Europe and Japan.

Every once in a while you will hear about people who made a fortune by putting all their money into one investment. You hear all about the people who became rich by owning Microsoft from the initial public offering or IPO, when the company was first made available for people to buy a part of it. You don't hear from all the people who owned stocks in one of the hundreds of other computer manufacturers or the many software companies that went bankrupt in the '80s. Yes, some people have done very well by having all their eggs in one basket, but that is not the norm. Doing this exposes you to a tremendous amount of risk when it's not necessary.

What Is Asset Allocation?

Wise investments are not always the ones with the highest return. You might want the highest return, but are you willing to deal with the increased risk? Remember that the higher the potential returns, the higher the potential risk. The goal of any good diversification plan is to try to increase the potential for return while trying to minimize the risk involved. The key to this process is not putting all your eggs in one basket. The technical term is "asset allocation."

The most popular way to describe good asset allocation is through a pie analogy. Think of it as a pie made up of a variety of pieces. Each person's investment pie is made up differently. Rather than some slices of the pie being apple, pumpkin, peach, or cherry, think of the pieces being stocks, bonds, and foreign stocks. You might also have a piece of real estate and a small slice of cash or precious metals. How you make up your pie depends on a couple of factors, such as your time horizon and how much risk you are willing to take and still be able to get a good night's sleep.

Why Should You Allocate Assets?

Asset allocation describes the percentages of different types of investments that make up your whole investment mix or portfolio. Why should you look at the whole mix of your investments rather than the individual securities that actually make the difference?

1. No matter how good a stock analyst you are (and let's face it, you are probably lousy), you cannot predict which piece of investment pie is going to do the best.

2. By putting together a mix of investments that work differently from each other, you will be able to reduce the volatility or the ups and downs of the value of your investments. A good mix of investments helps to level out the performance of the whole portfolio. It helps to minimize losses by putting together investments that do not move in the same direction.

3. It gives you an objective investment strategy to follow. Most of your mistakes in investing will come from making decisions based on how you feel rather than what you think. A study showed that over 92 percent of your

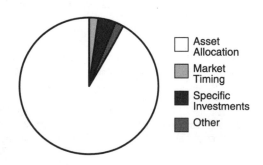

Asset Allocation

Market Timing

Specific Investments

Other

investment return will come from having the right mix of assets. Only 2 percent of your return will come from trying to time the market, about 4 percent return is based on the specific investments you choose, and another 2 percent is based on other factors. So 92 percent comes from thinking and at least 6 percent from feeling. How do most people invest? They focus on the feeling part and make a major investment mistake.

How Do I Allocate Assets?

There are many possible mixtures of investment types in an asset allocation because there are so many different types of investors and investor needs. Elderly people who live off their investments need to be conservative and want to preserve their principal, whereas young people have a much longer time horizon before they will need the money, so they can be more aggressive.

At this point you don't need to be concerned what specific types of investments should go into your mix, but that you have the right mix. Think of this part of the process as putting all the straight-edged pieces of a puzzle together so you have a framework for where to put all the other pieces. Establishing the right mix will provide you with the framework to build your investment strategy.

To start laying your puzzle's edges in place, you need to ask a few questions. First, how much time do you have before you need the investments? You may have several time horizons depending on your investment goals, although your risk tolerance probably will remain the same. For example, if you are investing for retirement, you probably have a thirty-year or more time horizon. But, for your investment to buy a house, you may have only a five-year horizon. Take the time to note your time horizons for a few of your investment goals.

The second question is about your risk level: How much can the value of your portfolio move up and down and you will still be able to sleep at night? For example, how comfortable would you be if you invested $1,000 and a year later it was only worth $800? Could you wait a year to see its value rise again? Is your risk comfort level low (I couldn't sleep; I need my investment principal intact), medium (I could sleep but not well; I need most of my investment principal intact), or high (I could sleep like a baby; I can wait for the economy to improve)?

Investment Goal	Time Horizon	Risk Comfort
e.g., Retirement	35 years	High: I could sleep

Your Mix

You can get much of the benefit of a diverse portfolio by having a very basic mix of stocks and bonds.

Three Major Asset Classes

1. *Stocks,* also known as equities, represent ownership in public corporations. Each stock is priced according to the perceived value of the corporation and its ability to generate profits in one of two ways: Dividends are a portion of these profits, and capital appreciation is recognized as an increase in the value of the stock.

2. *Bonds* are IOUs. When you buy a bond, you are lending money to a company or government agency. The borrower agrees to pay back the principal, along with a set rate of interest related to the risk involved. Bonds usually pay a higher interest rate than stock dividends and are used to generate current income.

3. *Cash* and cash equivalents include savings accounts, money market instruments, and certificates of deposit (CDs). These types of investments have the greatest relative safety but are unlikely to generate the increase you may need to reach your financial goals. They are good places to invest your money for your short-term needs.

Although you see three major asset classes, you need to be aware that inside the stock and bond asset classes there are many further ways to diversify. You might have a percentage of small company stocks since, historically, small companies have outperformed large companies by a percentage or two. If you add some international segments to your asset mix, you can take advantage of growth in overseas markets even if the domestic markets are down.

You should have some bonds in your portfolio since they act entirely differently from stocks (see chapters 5 and 6). A good bond mutual fund will give you the diversity among the many different types of bonds out there.

Determining Your Mix

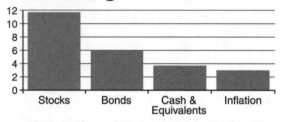

Annualized Returns 1925–1998 of Major Asset Classes

Let's go back now and look at the scores from your risk tolerance questionnaire in chapter 3 and see how they lead you to the next step in making your first investment.

The Conservative Investor

If your total score was less than 10 points, you are a conservative investor with a low tolerance for risk. You might consider investing 15

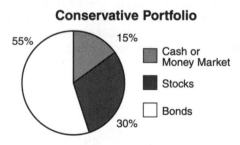

percent in cash equivalent or money market funds (see page 45 for more on these) and 55 percent in conservative bonds or bond mutual funds that seek to maintain the safety of your principal while seeking a steady stream of income. However, don't ignore the 30 percent in conservative stocks or stock mutual funds, as prudent investors will want to diversify appropriately.

The Moderate Investor

A score of 10 to 19 means you are a moderate investor. You can accept some degree of risk in search of potentially higher returns. A

Moderate Portfolio

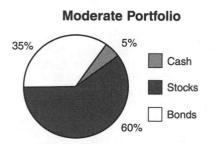

35% 5%
60%

- Cash
- Stocks
- Bonds

mix of stocks and bonds that emphasizes steady income along with the potential for some increase might be an appropriate investment. You could utilize a money market fund for your cash, and a mix of bonds or bond funds for your 35 percent bonds. With your stock portion representing 60 percent, you want to diversify it even further. You may want your stock portion to be made up of 50 percent large well-known companies, 30 percent smaller, rapidly growing companies, and 20 percent international companies. This divides the stock portion of your portfolio to provide greater diversity.

The Aggressive Investor

A score of 20 or more means you are an aggressive investor, comfortable with a higher degree of risk in pursuit of substantial rewards. Keep in mind that aggressive does not mean careless. As long as you are willing to "ride out" short-term fluctuations in the marketplace,

Aggressive Portfolio

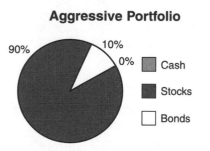

90% 10%
0%

- Cash
- Stocks
- Bonds

you should consider putting the bulk of your investment mix in stocks and stock funds that seek long-term increase. Since most of your investment dollars are in stocks, you need to diversify even further among different stock classes. In addition to 10 percent in bonds, your investment mix might include investing 25 percent in the international area, 15 percent in small growing companies, 10 percent in small value companies (ones that may have had better days), and 20 percent each in large growing and large value companies.

My Investment Strategy

It is time for you to start thinking about what kind of investor you are and what your investment pie might look like. Don't feel pressured into thinking you have to determine what your investment strategy might look like for the rest of your life because you will probably change it along the way. Just spend a couple of minutes jotting down your thoughts to the following (this is easier if you forget you are investing your first $100 and think big!).

My Time Horizon: _____ years

My Risk Tolerance: _____

Stocks: Total _____%

Big Growing Companies	_____%
Stock Mutual Funds	_____%
Small Growing Companies	_____%
Small Value Companies	_____%
International Companies	_____%
Large Value Companies	_____%

Bonds: Total _____%

Conservative Bonds	_____%
Bond Mutual Funds	_____%

Cash: Total _____%

CDs	_____%
Money Market	_____%
Savings Accounts	_____%

If you have different goals with different time horizons, you may want to do a few different mixes. Keep in mind that the shorter the time you have until you will need the money, the more conservative you should be with investments.

CHAPTER 5

Taking Stock of Stocks

"He's interviewing stock brokers. But wait until they hear how *little* he has to invest."

Taking Stock of Stocks

This chapter will focus on the details of stocks so you can get a better understanding of whether stocks should be included in your investment mix.

A Not-So-Bright Idea

Let's say you and a few friends want to start a business that makes moonglasses—you know, sunglasses for the night. In order to start this business you need to raise $100,000. Some of it will be used to develop lunar ray deflecting lenses and some will be used to buy machines that make the frames and, of course, some will be used to pay the workers. Since you and your friends have a combined total of $473.25 (including tips), you have a problem. The idea is great and your market research indicates that both of your aunts would love a pair of moonglasses. So you want to go ahead, but you need money.

What is the solution to your need for money? Take your company public, sell stock, and allow others to own a piece (or have a share) of Lunar Inc. by investing in it. You need $100,000, so you could sell 100,000 shares of Lunar Inc. for $1 each or 1,000 shares for $100 each or 10,000 shares for $10 each.

All of the shares represent an equal portion of ownership in the company. If 10,000 people each bought one share for $10, there would be 10,000 owners of the company. If an investor wanted to own more than 1/10,000 of the company, he or she could buy more shares at the initial public offering or IPO. If someone becomes a part owner of the company, he or she is issued a stock certificate that shows how many shares of the company he or she owns.

Let's assume sales of the first moonglasses are out of this world and your company is making lots of money. This means that the value of the shares of the company will go up. The shares that were first sold for $10 each to raise money for the start of the company are traded or bought and sold among people in the secondary market (where stock is bought and sold after the IPO) who want to own a piece of this incredible company. New investors may pay the original owners $12 or $15 for their shares in Lunar Inc. The company no longer gets any of this money, but the shareholders will benefit from selling their shares at a profit. On the other hand, if you find that there is not a market for moonglasses (just pretend!) and you don't sell very many, the stock price of Lunar Inc. may go down. The shareholders will not like that, so you have to figure out a way to improve sales or get your pizza uniform dry-cleaned quickly!

Welcome to Wall Street

The New York Stock Exchange, NYSE, on Wall Street in New York City is the best-known place in the world where people buy and sell stocks from each other. With the electronic age, the ability to buy and sell stocks is no longer limited to a physical location. There are a growing number of electronic exchanges where orders to buy and sell stock are matched up electronically. The most famous of these is the National Association of Security Dealers Automated Quotation System or NASDAQ. The NASDAQ lists stocks of companies in the growth sector like technology, telecommunications, and finance.

Hollywood and the news media have glamorized Wall Street and the stock market by giving the impression that everyone is making more money than they know what to do with. With over 50 percent of U.S. households invested in the stock market through mutual funds or individual stocks, it is important to understand that "being" in the stock market doesn't mean that you are going to make more money than you know what to do with. The stock market can be a dangerous place if you don't know what you are doing or if you don't do your homework. But it is a place where you can put some of your money to work for you.

The Benefits of Stocks

As you saw with Lunar Inc., stock represents ownership in a public company. A public company is a company that anyone can own a piece or all of, if they are willing to pay the price. The major benefit of stock ownership is that it gives you the opportunity to own a piece of a large company with limited liability. This means that if Lunar Inc. were to become hugely popular and successful, your share of the company would increase as well. On the other hand, if Lunar Inc. was sued because people wearing moonglasses started having more car wrecks, you are not responsible to pay all the lawsuits. If you invested $1,000 in the company and it was sued, the most you could lose is $1,000.

Splits, Capital Appreciation and Dividends, DRIPs, and Dollar Cost Averaging

Here are five terms you should be familiar with.

- *Splits*. With few exceptions, most common stocks trade for less than $100. As the price of a stock climbs closer to $100, the people who run the company may declare a stock split to bring the price of the stock down and make it more affordable for investors. Think of a stock split the same as changing money. You have a $10 bill and you exchange it for two $5 bills. You don't have any more money, but now you have twice as many bills. If a stock splits two for one, the same thing happens. If you owned 10 shares of Lunar Inc. at a cost of $100 before the split, after the split you would own 20 shares at $50.

- *Capital Appreciation and Dividends*. There are two basic ways in which owning a stock is going to make money. The first way is that the value people are willing to pay for the stock goes up. This is usually because the company is making more money and each piece of ownership or company share is increasing. If you bought Lunar Inc. at $10 and now people are willing to buy it for $20, you have seen your investment appreciate $10 or 100 percent.

  The second way owning a stock can make money for you is through dividends. A company that is making money has a choice to put all the profit back into the company or to distribute some of the profit to the shareholders or owners. This is called a dividend.

  Financial, pharmaceutical, and utility companies are good examples of the type of companies that usually give dividends. If Lunar Inc. stock was worth $25 and the board of directors approved a $1.25 dividend per share, each shareholder would get a check for $1.25 per share or the chance to reinvest that amount in more shares of Lunar Inc. This process is called dividend reinvestment.

- *DRIPs*. Many companies have an easy way to buy their stock and reinvest the dividends. They are called dividend reinvestment programs and are a great way for the new investor to get started in stocks. If you are determined to start off with stocks, you should know about DRIP programs. They are free programs to encourage people to invest in a certain company. It doesn't mean the stocks are being given away, but it means it doesn't cost anything to buy or sell them, and you can buy smaller portions than if you made the same purchase through a stockbroker. (A stockbroker is not supposed to make you go broke; he or she is licensed to buy and sell stock on your behalf.) DRIPs are available from over a thousand companies. They allow you to make periodic contributions to buy shares of a company with little or no commission or cost. In fact, over 100 companies will sell you their stock with a 3 to 10 percent discount below the current market price if you do it through a DRIP.

Most DRIPs allow investors to send in optional cash payments as low as $10. This lets you buy a fraction of a share. For example, if you are investing in Lunar Inc., which has stock selling for $30, and you send in $15, you buy half a share. A DRIP is a great way to get started in investing in stocks for a reasonable price, and it allows you to take advantage of dollar cost averaging.

- *Dollar Cost Averaging.* If the main goal of investing is to buy low and sell high, dollar cost averaging is going to make sure you never buy all your stock at the highest price. One of the most difficult things for investors is to buy when their investments are down, but this may be the best time to buy. With dollar cost averaging, DCA, you are going to buy sometimes when the price is up, but you also buy when the price is down.

You need to remember that dollar cost averaging does not guarantee you will make a profit. It takes advantage of the volatility, the ups and downs, of the stock price. If you continue to invest in an investment that keeps going down, then you will not see a profit. This is a strategy that you need to employ over a couple of years at least. When you are young and just starting out in buying stocks, DCA is probably the best way to go.

How to Buy and Sell Stock

If you want to buy stock or sell stock, you can't just look at e-Bay and see what you can get for it. All orders must go through a regulated exchange like the NYSE, which is not much different from e-Bay. All that an exchange does is bring together buyers and sellers of stock. Stock grouped with other stocks also can be bought and sold. The most popular way of doing this is through mutual funds, which you will learn about in chapter 7. The benefit of these grouped investments is that it takes the pressure off of picking just the right stock. Regardless of whether you buy stocks individually or grouped together, you have to take some basic steps to make it happen.

1. *Find a Stock Broker.* You have to have a broker in order to execute a stock trade. In order to keep people from being taken advantage of, there are strict rules that are enforced for people who trade stocks. In other words, you can't decide that you want to be a stockbroker and begin trading stocks without the proper training and licensing. You can find two major types of brokers who can help you trade a stock.

   a. *A full-service broker* will provide research, advice, and a variety of other financial services. For this service you will pay more to have your trade executed. The trade happens when you call your broker at Merrill Lynch, Paine Webber, or Prudential Securities, to list a few, with your instructions. Full-service brokers have a legal duty to make sure that any trades they do are suitable for the client.

   b. *A discount broker* is set up to give you the bare-bones services. This means that your order will be executed through their firm but you will not get any extensive advice or service. You can access a discount broker by calling one on the phone or accessing a Web site for an online broker. You will save money this way, but you are also on your own. For a beginner, trading online or with a discount broker is something to seriously consider. Companies like Charles Schwab, E*TRADE, and Ameritrade are some of the best-known online brokers.

2. *Open an Account.* Before you conduct a trade with a broker, you will need to open an account. There are different types of accounts you can open—the most common being a cash account. This works very similar to a checking account. You deposit money into the account, and then you can buy stock up to the value you have deposited. If you open an account with $500, you can buy $500

worth of stock. If you already have a stock certificate as a result of a gift or inheritance, you can deposit it into this account as well.

3. *Execute the Order to Buy or Sell.* In order to execute a trade, you are going to need three pieces of information: (1) The name of the company or its ticker symbol—a unique one to four letter abbreviation of the company—for your broker; (2) whether you are making a buy or a sell order; (3) any special instructions for when or at what price you want the transaction to take place.

Frequent Trader Beware!

Over the last few years, with the growth of discount brokers and online trading, the tendency has been for some investors to over-trade their accounts. The phrase "day trader" has become part of our modern vocabulary. The goal of these investors is to try to trade in and out of a stock on a daily basis in an attempt to time the high and the low price of the stock. This strategy may seem enticing, especially in a long, rising market, but it is dangerous—as many day traders saw in the year 2000. Research shows that the households that trade more frequently do worse than the households that trade infrequently.

Trading costs you money, and the tendency is to sell when you should be buying and buy when you should be selling. This book is about a long-term investment strategy and strongly discourages you from anything remotely related to day trading.

How to Read a Stock Table

Go to the business section of your newspaper and you will find tables of information regarding most popular stocks.

1	2	3	4	5	6
52-Week High	52-Week Low	Stock	Div	Yield %	P/E Ratio
47½	10	LUNR	1.25	5	16

7	8	9	10	11
Vol. 100s	High	Low	Close	Net Change
25	26¼	24½	25	+ 1¼

What It Means

- *Columns 1, 2, 3*—During the last 52 weeks, stock of Lunar Inc. sold for a high of $47.50 and a low of $10.
- *Column 4*—LUNR is the ticker symbol for Lunar Inc. Its stock pays $1.25 dividend per share yearly.
- *Column 5*—Based on today's price of $25 and dividend of $1.25, the investor will receive a 5 percent return. The yield is obtained by dividing the annual dividend by the closing price.
- *Column 6*—At today's price, the ratio of the price of the stock to earnings per share of the stock is 16. By looking at the P/E ratio, you can compare different companies in the same industry. Generally, low P/E stocks tend to have higher dividend yields and less risk. You get the P/E ration by dividing the stock price by the company's latest 12 months' earnings per share.
- *Column 7*—2,500 shares of Lunar Inc. changed hands on this day.
- *Columns 8, 9, 10, 11*—During the trading day, the price was as high as $26.25 and as low as $24.50. The final price was $25, which was $1.25 more than the final price the day before.

Now It's Your Turn

Find five companies you are interested in and look them up in the paper. Locate their "ticker symbol" and find what price their stock currently is. After that, find out what it traded for a year ago and, if possible, five years ago. Then ask yourself how these stocks might fit in your investment pie. A hint to finding this information: Look in the finance section of the newspaper or, even better, look under the finance section of Yahoo, AOL, MSN, or other Internet sources.

Company Name	Ticker Symbol	Current Stock Price	Stock Price 1 Year Ago	Stock Price 5 Years Ago

CHAPTER 6

Bond Basics

Bond Basics

If stocks are the part of investments that everyone thinks is exciting and exhilarating, bonds are the investments that everyone needs to bring them back to reality. The amount of money in bonds and other fixed-income securities makes the money in the stock market look like pocket change. The reason? Simple. Bonds, although less potent when it comes to returns, are almost solid as a rock when it comes to volatility. You can hear how stocks have outperformed bonds over time all you want, but if you can't sleep at night because your stocks are down 35 percent, what is the benefit? Don't misunderstand. Bonds also fluctuate in value, just not as much as stocks and for different reasons.

What Are Bonds?

Lunar Inc. has had a stellar year with several models of moonglasses coming to market and selling very successfully. Rather than just sitting and enjoying your new position as the Chief Executive Officer (CEO) of Lunar Inc., you want to take the company to new heights.

Where do you get more money? You have two options. One is to issue more stock in a secondary offering, like you did in the IPO. The problem with this solution is that it will dilute or reduce the original shareholders' ownership in Lunar Inc. The stockholders may not like that and, since you can't find your pizza uniform, you look at the second option for raising money for the expansion.

The second option is to issue bonds. Bonds are loans made to companies, corporations, or the government. In return for loaning money to these institutions, the investor gets interest. If Lunar Inc. were to issue 50 bonds for $1,000 each, that would bring in the $50,000 needed for expansion and not upset the current stockholders.

The reason investors are interested in these bonds is because Lunar Inc. promises to pay back the lender the full value of the bond on a set date *and* pay a set interest rate each year until then. In this case, let's say Lunar Inc. issued a five-year bond with a 10 percent interest rate. This means that if you owned one Lunar Inc. bond, you would receive 10 percent interest on your $1,000 investment each year, or $100. At the end of the fifth year, Lunar Inc.

would have paid you a total of $500 dollars and given you your $1,000 principal or initial investment back.

Bond Prices and Interest Rates

If an investor decides not to hold on to his or her bond for the full five years, he or she can sell it in a secondary market—but may not get the full $1,000 back. In order to keep every investor that buys Lunar Inc. bonds informed, the company needs to explain how the price of bonds and interests are related.

A typical bond would sell for $1,000, mature in five years, and have a coupon of 10 percent. They call it a coupon because if you have a physical bond certificate, you would have one coupon to tear off each year to get your interest. The 10 percent would be competitive in relationship to other current interest rates.

Now what would happen if, within a year, you wanted to sell your bond but current interest rates had gone up to 12.5 percent? You paid $1,000 for your bond with a 10 percent coupon, so it would pay $100 in interest for the year. Someone wanting to buy a new bond would still pay $1,000, but because of the rise in interest rates their bond would give them $125 for the year. The coupon rate for your bond is 10 percent, so the $100 per year interest income will not change, regardless of the price of the bond. To make your bond interest rate more competitive with the new bonds at 12.5 percent, you would need to sell it for a discount. If you sold it for $800 at a $200 loss and it paid $100 per year, the buyer of your bond would be getting 12.5 percent return (100 ÷ 800 = 12.5 percent). If the buyer held on to this bond, he or she would also get an additional $200 from the investment, since the bond when it matures is refunded at the original purchase price. In summary, as interest rates went up, the price of your bond went down.

Now what would happen if interest rates went down? Let's say that new bonds are being issued at 8 percent. If you had a bond that was paying $100 per year and the new bonds were paying $80 per year, your bond would go up in value, because investors would want the $100 in interest more than the $80. If you sold your bond for $1,200 with a 10 percent coupon, the buyer would be getting 8.3 percent (100 ÷ 1,200) current return. As the interest rate went down, the price of your bond went up.

Remember that if you hold the bond until it matures, you will get the full principal back. The fluctuation of prices is only important if you try to sell it before it matures. As a public company, Lunar Inc. can issue bonds or stocks to raise money.

In the case of governments trying to raise money, they cannot issue stock, since they cannot issue pieces of ownership to the highest bidder. It is either bonds or higher taxes when it comes to the government deciding what to do to raise more money.

Long or Short

Bonds have a life span that is fixed when they are issued. Typically bonds are characterized as long-term, intermediate-term, and short-term, depending on the time until they mature. A long-term bond is usually issued for thirty years or more (some for as much as one hundred years). Intermediate-term bonds usually mature in five to fifteen years, and short-term bonds mature in five or fewer years. The reason there are different lengths of maturity is that some people do not want to have to worry about their income, which is being paid to them from the bond interest, changing or fluctuating.

Let's say an investor received $100 from her 10 percent Lunar Inc. bond. Five years later the current interest is 5 percent. The investor has to take the $1,000 dollars they would receive from her matured bond and reinvest it at a lower rate. She would only get $50 a year now. When a bond matures, there is no guarantee that the current interest rate being paid by the issuer (company or government) will be the same as the old rate. So the investor might prefer to buy a bond that will provide her a stable income for, say, twenty years.

Bonds Do Have Risk

When we talk about the interest rate a bond pays, it is important to understand that the rate of interest it pays will not be the same for all bonds issued at the same time. Factors such as the issuing company's credit rating and the length to maturity of a bond will also affect the interest rate. Typically the longer the maturity of a bond, the higher the interest rate will be. Also, the riskier the issuing organization is considered to be, the higher the interest rate will be.

The main factor that affects bond rates is the credit rating of the issuing company or institution. The government of the United

States is considered to be the safest issuer of bonds as it would be the last issuer to ever default, or not pay, on a bond. Because the U.S. government is considered the safest place to lend money, the bonds it issues also pay the least amount of interest.

The other extreme of risk is found in what are commonly called junk bonds. These are issued by more speculative businesses to raise money. Since there is a greater risk that the issuer will not be able to make the interest payments or refund the initial purchase price of the bond, the issuer has to have a higher interest rate in order to attract investors. Between these two extremes are a variety of differently rated issuers of bonds, rated by various rating agencies. If a company has a lower credit rating, it will have to pay more to borrow money from you, the investor. Moody's and Standard & Poor's are the two main rating agencies of bonds.

Moody's	Standard & Poor's		
Aaa	AAA	Best Quality	Investment Grade
Aa	AA	High Quality	
A	A	High-Medium Quality	
Baa	BBB	Medium Quality	
Ba	BB	Some Speculation	
B	B	More Speculation	Speculative
Caa	CCC	Poor Quality	
Ca	CC	Highly Speculative	Junk Bonds
C	C	Poorest Quality	
D	•	In Default	

Lunar Inc. has an A rating and issues bonds at a 10 percent interest rate. If Moody's thought Lunar Inc. were a higher risk because of other debts, it may downgrade the company to B. If that were the case, Lunar Inc. may now have to issue bonds at a 12 percent interest, which will cost the company more money in interest payments. The goal of every company is to have a higher rating so it does not have to issue bonds with higher interest rates.

Government Bonds

In addition to the U.S. savings bonds and U.S. Treasuries mentioned in chapter 3, there are agency bonds and municipal bonds you should be aware of.

- *Agency Bonds.* One last investment area that the U.S. government is involved in indirectly is the area of agency bonds. Even though these agencies receive the support (in the form of money if needed) of the U.S. government, the government does not necessarily own them. These agencies, like the U.S. government, borrow money from investors. Like other debt instruments, such as bonds, these are IOUs that the lender is issuing for the use of the money borrowed.

  The three most commonly known agencies are the General National Mortgage Association (GNMA), the Federal Home Loan Mortgage Corporation (FHLMC), and the Federal National Mortgage Association (FNMA). You may know them by their nicknames Ginnie Mae, Freddie Mac, and Fannie Mae.

  These agency bonds trade just like other bonds: Their price moves in the opposite direction of interest rates. They are available through brokerage firms and may be brand-new issues to raise money or may be trading on the secondary market.

- *Municipal Bonds* are issued by state and local governments, with one major difference: They are federally tax free. That means that when you get your check for the bond interest, you do not have to pay federal tax on it like you would with U.S. government bonds. These types of bonds are usually best suited for people in high tax brackets. Since the rate of return is the same, the higher your tax bracket, the more you will save in taxes.

  Think of bonds as a great way to get your money working for you but with much less risk than the stock market. Since bond prices go up and down with interest rates and not with the profitability of the companies or governments issuing them, they add great diversity to stocks. The goal is not to have everything moving in the same direction. By combining bonds with your stocks, you can reduce the volatility of your investment's value as it increases to meet your goals.

CHAPTER 7

An Overview of Mutual Funds

An Overview of Mutual Funds

Imagine an investment that gave you great diversification, required a small initial amount to invest, could be as safe or risky as you wanted it to be, was cost-efficient, and had a professional money manager overseeing its day-to-day activity. If you think this is too good to be true, then think again. A mutual fund is all this and more. For the beginning investor there is probably no better investment available.

With as little as $250 you can begin to invest for the future. Mutual funds give you access to all the important factors of investing you have learned about so far, such as not putting all your eggs in one basket, risk management, and access to stocks and bonds.

What Is a Mutual Fund?

A mutual fund is an investment that pools many investors' dollars to buy appropriate stocks and bonds. A mutual fund owner owns a share of the pooled funds. These funds are managed by professional money managers who buy and sell the stocks or bonds of the fund based on their judgment of what will help the fund achieve its stated goals.

Imagine a mutual fund as a basket of stocks from fifty to one hundred companies or a basket of bonds from many different municipalities. A mutual fund manager who is looking for new, innovative, well-managed, and rapidly growing companies would come across Lunar Inc. right away. The manager would then determine if Lunar Inc. fits the mutual fund's profile. If it does, the mutual fund manager may buy as many shares of the company as he or she wants.

The fund manager may also buy several other companies' stock that day, in addition to selling others that the fund owns. The value of each share of the mutual fund is determined at the end of the day by adding up the value of all the stocks and bonds the fund owns and dividing by the number of issued shares. The value of each piece of this investment is based on the movement of many different companies. This helps to spread the risk beyond what just one company is doing.

Over the past fifteen years, the growth of mutual fund companies has exploded. Today there are over 10,000 different mutual funds available to invest in. Mutual funds are categorized in three major groups: stock funds, bond funds, and money market funds.

Each *mutual fund,* whether stock, bond, or money market, has a defined objective. Some funds are very aggressive, but others produce a current income stream through dividends and interest. Today you have a fund for almost anything. You have a fund that invests in just technology stocks or just financial stocks. Some mutual funds are designed around being socially conscious: These funds may not invest in tobacco or alcohol-related companies. It is this stated objective that helps you decide which fund or combination of mutual funds you should be in.

Bond funds allow you to have a diversified bond portfolio with just one small initial investment. Many individual bonds are not available for less than $5,000, but through a mutual fund you can buy a piece of over fifty to one hundred bonds for $1,000 or less. Some bond funds may focus on corporate bonds; others may be just made up of Treasury bonds. Many mutual fund companies have bond funds made up of just municipal bonds from a certain state in order to take advantage of their tax-free status.

Money market mutual funds are like savings accounts. For every dollar you put in, you get one dollar out plus the interest that is being generated. The risk of losing money is very small, so many investors prefer this to stock or bond funds. The rate of return on money market funds will be similar to short-term interest rates, so when the rates are low, the return will be low. Many money market accounts allow check writing and have become popular alternatives to savings accounts because of the much better interest rate they provide.

Load or No-Load, That Is the Question

With so many mutual funds out there, how do you know which ones to use and how to buy them? Investing in mutual funds is not hard. You can purchase load and no-load funds from a brokerage firm, discount broker, or online broker as well as from many banks and savings institutions. Load funds have a sales charge; no-load funds do not charge the shareholders any sales fees.

Why pay for some funds if you can buy others with no sales charge? Why do some people change their own oil and others pay someone to do it? When you invest in a mutual fund with a sales charge, you get additional service and help from someone who deals with mutual funds every day. These money professionals can help you pick the right funds for your need. They can also tell you if a particular fund has Lunar Inc. as one of its stock holdings.

It is important to know that in all mutual funds there are other fees and expenses besides sales fees. All the information that you need to know about a mutual fund is contained in what is called "the prospectus." This document educates you on the important elements of a mutual fund. The Securities and Exchange Commission, or SEC, closely regulates the information mutual funds put out to make sure it is truthful and accurate.

Regular Fees

All mutual funds are in the business of making money so they have to charge the shareholders in some way. A summary of fees and expenses appear in the fund's prospectus near the beginning. The fees can range from less than 1 percent to as high as 5 to 8 percent depending on the type of fund. A good site to look up the true cost of a mutual fund is *www.personalfund.com*. Just type in the symbol or abbreviation for the mutual fund, and, presto, it is there. Here are some of the main categories you will see.

- *Management fees* are the expenses charged annually to administer the fund. This is what you pay to have a professional money manager decide when to buy and sell stocks or bonds in your portfolio rather than doing it yourself. The fee can vary from less than half of 1 percent to close to 2 percent. Bond funds typically have the least management fees; international equity funds have the highest.

- *Distribution fees,* also referred to as 12b-1 fees, cover the marketing and advertising expenses. Sometimes these fees also are used to pay bonuses to employees and the sales people who sell the funds. Not all funds charge these fees, but they can range from one quarter of 1 percent to 1 percent for the funds that do.

- *Redemption fees.* In order to discourage frequent trading, these fees are charged by some mutual fund companies when you sell shares.

Not all expenses need to be reported in a mutual fund's prospectus. One fee that cannot be determined beforehand is the cost of trading the stocks in and out of the fund. Because of the high volume of stock trades that are done by mutual fund companies, the cost of trading is much less than if you tried to do it yourself, but it still costs money. An aggressive fund that trades often will have a higher expense than one that buys and holds stocks longer. This cost can often amount to 1 to 2 percent.

Sales Charges

This is probably the area least understood by mutual fund buyers. Sales charges are in addition to all the fees mentioned above. If you choose to pay a sales charge to someone for helping you pick your mutual funds, you need to know how the costs work. Sales charges fall into three categories: front-end load, back-end load, and level load. Each has its advantages and disadvantages.

Front-end load funds have a sales charge at the time of purchase, typically from 2 to 5.75 percent. The more money you invest, the less the sales charge is. This fund has more costs up front, but the person who holds on to his or her fund for over five years usually comes out ahead because front-load funds are the most cost-efficient with annual management fees. If you invested $1,000 in a mutual fund with a 5 percent sales charge, you would end up investing $950.

A *back-end load* fund will not cost you a sales fee up front, but it will have higher internal annual management expenses, and you may be charged a penalty for leaving the fund early, usually within the first five years. You are also charged an extra 1 percent in management fees per year for up to five to seven years. The main advantage to this sales structure is that all of your initial investment amount gets working for you right away.

A *level-load* fund has little or no up-front charge, with little or no exit penalty, but it does carry an additional 1 percent annual management expense. The main advantage to this structure is that it gives you more flexibility of getting in and out of the fund with little or no penalty for changing your mind.

If you plan to pick your own funds, your options will also include funds that have no sales charge or *no-load* funds. These are designed for the do-it-yourself investor.

A Few Tips on Picking the Right Funds

With over 10,000 different mutual funds to choose from, how do you know which ones are best for you? A lot of people look for the fund that had the best performance in the previous year. But seldom does a fund that has a huge return one year repeat that performance the next year. It is best to select the proper fund or funds mix based on the time you have before you need the money and the risk level with which you are comfortable. You can look up a variety of Web sites like *www.yahoo.com, www.morningstar.com, www.fundspot.com,* and *www.zacks.com* that will allow you to evaluate funds. Here are a few things to consider when researching mutual funds.

1. *Look for good managers.* Mutual funds are professionally managed portfolios of stocks and bonds. More important than the mutual fund company or even last year's performance is the managers. These are the people who choose when to buy and sell the securities that make up your mutual fund. You want to know who they are and how long they have been doing their job.

2. *Look for a proven track record.* With the start of so many new mutual funds, many do not have any type of track record. With an economic cycle lasting five to seven years, it is impossible to tell how well a fund will do without a five- and preferably ten-year track record. You do not have to stay away from new funds, but look for new funds that are managed by people with a long track record with another fund to see how they have performed.

3. *Look for consistency.* When you look for the performance of a mutual fund, realize that one good year can hide a lot of bad years. Look beyond the three- or five-year performance numbers at how the fund performed each year. If the results are all over the map, you may want to keep looking.

4. *Look for risk level.* The higher the potential returns, the higher the potential risk. If a fund has had very high returns, you need to see how much risk is being taken to achieve those returns. Funds are usually categorized by rating companies as "below market risk," "market risk," and "above market risk." Your return should be consistent with the risk taken.

5. *Look for performance in comparison to a peer group.* Mutual funds are ranked against other mutual funds that are similar. See how the funds you are looking at compare with their peer group for the history of the fund and during different economic periods.

Mutual funds provide instant diversification, professional money managers, and dollar cost averaging—all for a reasonable price. As a new investor who plans to get involved in stocks or bonds, this is an area you should explore further. Most mutual fund companies have Web sites that allow you to explore the details of their funds, as well as to compare them with others. Once you get started with your mutual fund, you can look up how it is doing on their Web site or in the newspaper. Here is a general overview of what to look for when reviewing your fund.

How to Read a Mutual Fund Quote

1	2	3	4
Blackhawk Invt.	NAV	Net Chg	YTD % Ret
High Flyer Fund	43.50	+0.41	+ 10.3
Grounded Fund	22.65	- 0.12	+3.1

- *Column 1*—High Flyer Fund and Grounded Fund are part of the Blackhawk Investment Fund Family. A fund family is just a group of mutual funds managed by the same company.
- *Column 2*—The NAV stands for Net Asset Value per share of the fund at the close of the previous business day. Funds' NAVs are calculated by adding up the value of all the stocks and other securities owned by the fund, less any liabilities, and divided by the number of shares outstanding. The higher the value, the better the fund is doing.
- *Column 3*—The net change shows the change in the NAV from the previous day's quote. The High Flyer was up 41 cents and the Grounded Fund was down 12 cents.
- *Column 4*—YTD% Ret refers to the year-to-date percentage change in the value of the fund. This includes all distributions and reinvestments of dividends minus annual expenses.

Now It's Your Turn

So far you have taken a lot of steps toward your first investment. This next step will bring you to the investments you will probably start with. Use one of the following fund family Web sites to look up what each family has in the way of types of funds.

AIM—*http://www.aimfunds.com*
American Century Investments—*http://www.americancentury.com*
American Express/IDS—*http://finance.americanexpressfunds.com*
American Funds—*http://www.americanfunds.com*
Dreyfus—*http://www.dreyfus.com*
Evergreen—*http://www.evergreenfunds.com*
Fidelity—*http://www400.fidelity.com*
Franklin—*http://www.franklin-templeton.com*
INVESCO—*http://www.invescofunds.com*
Janus—*http://ww3.janus.com*
Prudential—*http://www.prudential.com*
Putnam Investments—*http://www.putnaminv.com*
Scudder—*http://www.scudder.com*
T. Rowe Price—*http://www.troweprice.com/*
Vanguard Group—*http://www.vanguard.com/*

Type of Fund	Fund Symbol		
1. Large Growth Fund	_____	_____	_____
2. Large Value Fund	_____	_____	_____
3. Small Growth Fund	_____	_____	_____
4. Small Value Fund	_____	_____	_____
5. International Fund	_____	_____	_____
6. Bond Fund	_____	_____	_____
7. Asset Allocated Fund	_____	_____	_____

(one that is a bit of all the above)

Now look up the symbols on Yahoo, Morningstar, or Zacks and see what you can find out about each fund in regard to the five things mentioned above that you should look for when researching a mutual fund.

CHAPTER 8

Tax Deferral and Govern- ment Freebies

"She's not taking any chances with our IRAs."

Tax Deferral and Government Freebies

By now you are probably feeling like an investment genius—ready to put your wisdom and knowledge to work for the betterment of society and your net worth. Sorry to burst your bubble, but you still have a few more things to learn.

The last piece of the puzzle that needs to be added before you can begin to build the perfect portfolio is tax deferral and government freebies. These two concepts need to be used in harmony with the knowledge you have already absorbed on understanding risk, asset allocation, and the main investment types.

Tax Deferral

Tax deferral is all about helping your investments to increase without paying current taxes on them. You need to understand that when a typical investment increases each year, whether through dividends and interest or through capital appreciation, you have some tax issues to address. Take a certificate of deposit (CD) that you put $1,000 into for one year that pays 10 percent interest. At the end of the year you would have earned $100, which you now have to pay taxes on before reinvesting your money in another investment. If you paid 30 percent tax, then you would have $70 to add to your $1,000 dollars of original principal ($1,000 + $100 - $30). You now have $1,070 to reinvest. If you take the same CD and put it into a tax-deferred account, you would not have to pay the $30 in tax and would have $1,100 to reinvest. Over time, the compounding effect on this difference is huge.

Keep in mind that tax deferred does not mean tax free. If the government allows you to increase your investment tax deferred, then the government will want the taxes on the increase when you begin to spend the money that has been growing tax deferred. The benefit of this is that your money works harder for you because you do not have to give up to 39.6 percent in federal tax, plus state and local tax, to the government as you realize or receive the increase each year. This means that the money you would have given to the government in taxes is still working for you to make more money.

Government Sponsored Retirement Plans

As a way to encourage Americans to save for their own retirement needs, the U.S. government has established some laws that encourage people to set aside money for the future. Although these plans were designed to encourage retirement savings, there are some incentives for first-time home buyers and those seeking higher education.

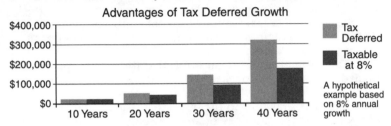

Advantages of Tax Deferred Growth

Tax Deferred

Taxable at 8%

A hypothetical example based on 8% annual growth

These laws focus on the ways to establish tax-advantaged savings and investments accounts. Tax advantaged is just a fancy way of saying that your investments can be tax deferred.

The Basics of Traditional and Roth IRAs

Individual retirement accounts or *IRAs* were established as an incentive for people to save for retirement. You need to realize that you can put a variety of investments into an IRA, such as CDs, money market funds, mutual funds, stocks, bonds, or any combination of these. Think of an IRA as a basket. Everything you put in the basket is tax deferred. Although there are exceptions, the maximum benefit of an IRA is realized when you make regular contributions each year and don't try to use the money until after age 59. If you try to take the money out before you reach 59, you have to pay a 10 percent penalty. Also, the money you take out must be considered regular income for the year in which you take it out, and it is taxed accordingly. If you were 60 years old or any age older than 59 and made $40,000 this year and took out $10,000 from your IRA, you would report to the IRS that you made $50,000 but you would not have to pay the 10 percent penalty. Not all people qualify to put cash in one of these tax-advantaged IRAs. Depending on your age, income, and the extent that you are covered by an employer-sponsored retirement plan, you may or may not be able to contribute to an IRA. For most first-time investors, however, this is a very viable option, and it is probably available to you.

There are two big advantages to an IRA. First, you can deduct your contributions to your IRA from your taxable income. Let's say you made $30,000 in income last year. On your tax return you need to declare that you made $30,000. That's pretty straightforward. If you contributed the current annual maximum amount to your IRA for a single person ($2,000), then you would only pay taxes on $28,000. That is a savings of $560 in taxes for someone in the 28 percent tax bracket.

The second big plus to an IRA is that the $2,000 you contributed will now be tax deferred. The chart on page 53 shows how powerful tax deferral can be, especially over the long run.

The main drawback to the IRA is that when you do take money out of it you must pay ordinary income tax on that amount.

Beginning in the tax year 1998, *Roth IRA*s came into being. The main difference between a traditional IRA and a Roth IRA is when they are taxed. A traditional IRA is not taxed on the way into the account and is tax deductible in the tax year it is deposited. The Roth IRA is not tax deductible (that is, it is money that has already been taxed) when you deposit it, but it is tax deferred and is not taxed when you withdraw the money. For young people in a lower tax bracket, this is an excellent way to get an early start on saving for retirement because it is likely that you will be in a higher tax bracket later in your career than when you first start working.

Employer/Employee-Sponsored Plans

The other main retirement gift from the government comes in the form of employer/employee incentives. Gone are the days when most big companies set up a nice pension for you to draw on when you retired. What has taken the pension's place in popularity are plans such as the 401(k). This plan allows eligible employees to defer from their paycheck even more money than an IRA. Again, think of a 401(k) as a basket that employees can put some of their earnings into and invest in a variety of investments. There are three main advantages to participating in a 401(k) when you're eligible.

1. The first is the *tax break* you get by contributing some of your paycheck to this account. Your contributions to a 401(k) allow you to reduce your taxable income by the amount that you contribute. In the year 2000 you could contribute up to $10,500, which is considerably more than the $2,000 of an IRA. If you earn $30,000 dollars a year and put $5,000 into your 401(k), you pay taxes on only $25,000. This is a savings of $1,400 in taxes that you would have had to pay. So you contribute $5,000 and the government gives you $1,400 back in the form of less taxes. Not bad. Keep in mind that the government will eventually get some taxes when you begin to spend that savings, but until then they are letting you deduct it from your current taxes.

2. The second major benefit is that you have *tax deferral* on your investment increase, just like in your IRA. This allows you to increase your deferred money free of current income tax.

3. The third major benefit of a 401(k) is that most plans include an *employer matching portion*. Every 401(k) is unique, but it is not unusual for employers to allow you to put up to 6 percent of your earnings into the plan tax deferred (with the maximum for the year 2000 of $10,500). In addition, many employers will match a certain portion of your contribution. For example, if you made $30,000 per year and had 6 percent of your income put in a tax-deferred 401(k) and your employer agreed to match 100 percent of the first 3 percent (this is how it is often worded), then you would see the following added to your 401(k) account: $1,800 from your own contribution, plus $900 from the employer. By contributing $1,800, you save $504 in taxes, plus you get an additional $900 added to your savings account. Of the $2,700 contributed to your account, $1,404, or over half, was a result of the kindness of Uncle Sam. It doesn't take a rocket scientist to see what a great opportunity a 401(k) can be. Several other types of retirement plans that are similar to a 401(k) plan are out there, so check and see what your current or future employer may provide and whether you may be eligible to participate in it.

When looking for a job, look for one that offers a 401(k) or one of the many other government sanctioned plans. Remember that there may be conditions of employment that must be fulfilled in order to participate in the plan and to have all the employer contributions credited to you.

Tax Deferral Investment Tip

Before leaving this chapter you need to understand the general rule of thumb when it comes to tax-advantaged investing. As you begin to set up your investment portfolio, now that all that money from Lunar Inc. is coming in, you need to do the following in respect to your long-term plans.

1. Try to first contribute the maximum to your work retirement plan that you are able. Different plans have different maximums, so check with your employer.

2. If you are able to do that, then put any additional investment dollars into an IRA up to the maximum, which is currently $2,000 per person per year.

3. Only after you have done these two should you begin to consider after-tax investments.

Now It's Your Turn

At this point, you need to follow up with two tasks. First, if you are currently working, find out if you have some sort of retirement plan through your employer. Ask to speak to your Human Resources manager or Plan Administrator. They will give you all the information you should need. If you are still in school or not currently employed, ask your parents or friends if you can research their company plan.

     Second, you need to find out what investments are available and what the details of the plans are, such as contribution limits and employee matching.

Retirement plan contact person	_____		
Type of company retirement plan	_____	_____	_____
Am I eligible to participate?	YES	NO	
Investments available	_____	_____	_____
Company match	_____	_____	_____

CHAPTER 9

Putting It All Together

"You know...now that we have an investment plan in place, maybe there's another *investment* we can start thinking about."

Putting It All Together

At this point you should be prepared to make your first investment. This chapter will take you through the final steps of how to put your first investment into action. Let's assume you have read the book and have accomplished the following.

1. Put in perspective the main purpose of investing, determined what percentage of your investment's return you would give away, and decided in general to whom you would give it.

2. Distinguished the difference between just saving your money and putting it to work for you.

3. Figured out a way to come up with a few investable dollars.

4. Understood that the goal of good investing is not to eliminate risk but to manage it. You also have determined your own risk tolerance.

5. Learned that 92 percent of your investment's return comes from having the right mix of assets, which can be objectively determined by looking at your risk tolerance. You have also designed a basic asset allocation and investment strategy for yourself that matches your time horizon and risk tolerance.

6. Became familiar with the basics of stocks, bonds, and mutual funds and did some research to find ones that are attractive to you.

7. Are ready to utilize tax-advantaged investing opportunities.

Making It Happen

Let's bring you to the point at which you have been able to put together a few investable dollars and want to put it to work for you in your first investment. You have discovered what type of investor you are and are comfortable with your risk level. Here is what to do next.

1. See if you are eligible for an employer/employee plan at work. If so, start putting a specific amount out of each paycheck into the investment choice or choices that fit your profile.

2. Do some research, ask around, and get some advice on good mutual funds and good financial advisors. Ask trusted friends or

successful family members who they use and if they might rec-
ommend that you use that person as well. You can look in your
Yellow Pages under finance/investing to see what local firms are
available. Your local bank may or may not provide investment
services. Ask at the information desk. Once you've selected the
person or firm, or made a short list of possibles, make an
appointment by phone to go and talk to that person or firm.
Take all the information you have come up with about your
investment wants and needs, risk tolerance, time horizon, and
so on, and go to the meeting prepared to ask lots of questions.
Most investment firms offer the same basic services.

3. Once you've found someone who has a track record you're
pleased with, whom you feel you can trust and with whom you
feel comfortable, take your investable dollars and open an
account with them.

A basic securities account is like a savings or checking
account at a bank except you deposit securities into it as well as
cash. If you buy stocks, bonds, or mutual funds, their value will
be included in your account statement each month.

As you open your account, you should be asked the typical
background questions relating to your prior investment experi-
ence to make sure he knows your situation and can make suitable investment recommendations. Make sure you read through
or have explained any detailed documents you have to sign.

Most securities accounts have a basic annual fee of around $50
but the minimum needed to open an account varies from firm to
firm. Some will allow you to start an account with only $1 but
$250 should be considered enough to get started in a good mutual
fund. Once your account is open, deposit your investable money
into it so it's there ready to buy your mutual funds, stocks, or
bonds. Finally, simply place your order verbally with your new
broker or online and buy 10 shares of Lunar Inc. or some type of
mutual fund. And you're on your way as a real investor.

4. Open up a retirement account with your bank, online, with a brokerage in town, or through some other financial institution that
can open such an account. If your bank doesn't provide these services, they may still be able to open a retirement account with a
Certificate of Deposit or CD. You can also look online for online

brokers such as E*TRADE, Ameritrade, or TD Waterhouse.

5. Begin to make systematic deposits in the fund or funds that represent your investment mix.

6. Continue to keep your time frame and goals in mind and do not lose sight of your objective strategies.

7. Allocate your return to giving and reinvesting as you have determined.

Reminders and Resources

1. *Don't get bogged down in the detail.* On any given day on financial TV and in money magazines, you can hear dozens of opinions on which way the stock market is going to go and which are the best stocks to buy. It's best to look at the strategies and time periods that stretch beyond the last couple of years or even the last decade. You want to be informed about how investments and strategies have performed and behaved over different economic cycles. What has happened during the last year or the last few years is not the way things have always been and always will be.

   When looking for good resources, look for those that are as unbiased as possible. A magazine for mutual funds published by a specific mutual fund company will push that company's funds.

   Newsletters are a good source of basic advice but tend to be expensive and not as user-friendly as many of the good Web sites that are available. One noncommercial magazine that has developed a high level of respect because of its ethics and integrity over the years is *Consumer Report*.

2. *Select good counsel.* As you begin your investment life, you will want to talk to people and seek counsel from those you trust. When it comes to getting investment advice, make sure you check out the following.

   a. *Track Record.* Proverbs 21:5 says, "The plans of the diligent lead to profit." A good test of a counselor's expertise is past performance.

   b. *References.* Few people ask for multiple references from a financial counselor and even fewer verify those references. Proverbs 21:29 says, "A wicked man puts up a bold front."

Most so-called advisors count on a good front in hopes of satisfying clients. Check their references thoroughly.

Remember in all of this to pray for wisdom and commit not only your life but your finances to God.

Web sites

The following Web sites contain a variety of investment information and advice from many different perspectives.

Alliance for Investor Education—*http://www.investoreducation.org*

CNBC—*http://www.cnbc.com*

Crown Financial Ministries (a merger of Christian Financial Concepts and Crown Ministries)—*http://www.crown.org/*

Investor Protection Trust—*http://www.investorprotection.org*

Jump$tart Coalition for Personal Financial Literacy—*http://www.jumpstartcoalition.org*

Morningstar—*http://www.morningstar.com*

National Association of Investors Corporation (NAIC)—*http://www.better-investing.org*

National Association of Securities Dealers, Inc. (NASD)—*http://www.nasd.com*

National Fraud Information Center—*http://www.fraud.org*

National Institute for Consumer Education (NICE)—*http://www.emich.edu/public/coe/nice*

The New York Stock Exchange—*http://www.nyse.com*

Personal Fund—*http://www.personalfund.com*

Sound Mind Investing (SMI)—*http://www.soundmindinvesting.com*

U.S. Department of Treasury—*http://www.publicdebt.treas.gov/sav/sav.htm*

Zacks—*http://www.zacks.com*

Glossary

Bond: Certificate representing a loan of money to a corporation or government for a specific period, in exchange for a promise to repay the bondholder the amount borrowed plus interest. In other words, an IOU.

Broker: A person who handles your orders to buy and sell securities.

Compound interest: Interest earned on interest.

Coupon rate: Fixed annual interest rate quoted when a bond is issued.

Diversification: Spreading investment funds among different types of investments and industries.

Dividend: Payment from a company's earnings to its stockholders.

Dollar cost averaging: Investing the same fixed dollar amount in the same investment at regular intervals over a long period of time.

Financial planner: A person who advises others about financial issues.

Full-service brokers: People who buy and sell securities or commodities for investors and offer information and advice.

Inflation: A general rise in prices of goods and services. It means that as prices go up, your money buys less.

Interest: The payment received from a financial institution, corporation, or government organization for lending money to it.

IRA: Individual Retirement Account, a tax-deferred savings account.

Junk bonds: High risk bonds issued by corporations with questionable ability to pay you back.

Load fund: A mutual fund purchased directly by you that charges a sales commission when bought.

Mutual fund: A company that invests the pooled money of its shareholders in various types of investments.

NASDAQ: The world's largest screen-based stock market built totally out of telecommunications networks and computers.

No-load fund: A mutual fund purchased directly by you that does not have a charge for buying it.

Portfolio: The total investments held by an individual.

Prospectus: Legal document describing an investment offered for sale.

Risk: The uncertainty that you will get an expected return.

Risk tolerance: A person's capacity to endure market price swings in an investment.

Rule of 72: A mathematical tool used to determine the length of time needed to double an investment at a given interest rate.

Savings: Money set aside to meet future needs with very little risk to principal or interest.

Securities: A broad range of investment instruments, including stocks, bonds, and mutual funds.

Stock: An investment that represents ownership in a company, also known as a share.

Tax-exempt investments: Investments that are not subject to tax on income earned.

Index